TATE PRICE

Simple Dividend Investing

Passive Income Through Dividends

Copyright © 2024 by Tate Price

All rights reserved. No part of this publication may be reproduced, stored or transmitted in any form or by any means, electronic, mechanical, photocopying, recording, scanning, or otherwise without written permission from the publisher. It is illegal to copy this book, post it to a website, or distribute it by any other means without permission.

Tate Price asserts the moral right to be identified as the author of this work.

Tate Price has no responsibility for the persistence or accuracy of URLs for external or third-party Internet Websites referred to in this publication and does not guarantee that any content on such Websites is, or will remain, accurate or appropriate.

Designations used by companies to distinguish their products are often claimed as trademarks. All brand names and product names used in this book and on its cover are trade names, service marks, trademarks and registered trademarks of their respective owners. The publishers and the book are not associated with any product or vendor mentioned in this book. None of the companies referenced within the book have endorsed the book.

First edition

This book was professionally typeset on Reedsy.
Find out more at reedsy.com

Contents

1	Welcome to The Simple Dividend Investing Guide.	1
2	Welcome!	5
3	How do Dividends Work	9
4	What is a Brokerage account?	12
5	What is passive income?	22
6	How to find stocks that pay dividends:	28
7	Dividend Kings and Aristocrats	36
8	The Power of Compound Interest	43
9	Self-Directed Investors	49
10	Resources that may help you in your investment journey.	53
11	Conclusion:	55

1

Welcome to The Simple Dividend Investing Guide.

I'm a lifelong investor excited to share my experiences and knowledge with you through this book. As we go along, we will discuss many aspects of investing and the stock market, and I will do my best to break everything down into simple and easily understandable steps.

I remember starting to learn about investing and the stock market. Everywhere I looked, information was available, but it was so complicated. It took years, but eventually, I understood how the stock market worked, how companies paid dividends, how to find and buy stocks that pay dividends, and how to manage a tax-friendly portfolio through qualified dividends.

Investing in dividend stocks may not be a quick path to wealth, but it can be a rewarding journey. By starting early and investing consistently, you can significantly boost your retirement income. And if you have a substantial amount to invest, it could even pave the way for an early retirement. I firmly believe that with the right knowledge and experience, anyone can build a reasonably safe and well-diversified portfolio.

I've always heard the expression KISS (Keep It Stupid Simple). In short, you should avoid unnecessary complexity and confusion in any design or plan. We will discuss this later in the book, and I will give you some examples of how I keep my investment portfolio simple and easily understandable.

While this book is not financial or investment advice (We'll get to this in a minute), I do hope to give you easily understandable, step-by-step knowledge of how the stock market and dividends work, so that you will be able to better discuss these topics with your financial/investment advisor.

Disclaimer:

Not legal advice

The information provided in this book is for general purposes only and is not an alternative to legal advice from your lawyer, other professional services provider, or expert. It is not intended to provide legal advice or opinions of any kind. You should not act or refrain from acting based solely upon the information provided in this book without first seeking appropriate legal or other professional advice. If you have any specific questions about any legal matter, you should consult your lawyer, other professional services provider, or expert. You should never delay seeking legal advice, disregard legal advice, or commence or discontinue any legal action because of the information in this book. The information in this book is provided for your convenience only. This information may have no evidentiary value and should be checked against official sources before it is used for any purposes. It is your responsibility to determine whether this information is admissible in a given judicial or administrative proceeding and whether there are any other evidentiary or filing requirements. Your use of this information is at your own risk.

Not financial advice:

The information in this book is provided for your convenience only and is not intended to be treated as financial, investment, tax, or other advice. Nothing contained in this book constitutes a solicitation, recommendation, endorsement, or offer by the author, their agents, employees, contractors, or any affiliated companies to buy or sell any securities or other financial instruments. All content in this book is information of a general nature and does not address the circumstances of any particular individual or entity. Nothing in this book constitutes professional and/or financial advice, nor does any information in this book constitute a comprehensive or complete statement of the matters discussed or the law relating thereto. You alone assume the sole responsibility of evaluating the merits and risks associated with the use of any information or other content in this book before making any decisions based on such information. You agree not to hold the author, its agents, employees, contractors, or any affiliated companies liable for any possible claim for damages arising from any decision you make based on the information made available to you through this book.

Not investment advice:

All investments are highly speculative in nature and involve substantial risk of loss. We encourage everyone to invest very carefully. We also encourage investors to get personal advice from their professional investment advisor and to make independent investigations before acting on the information found in this book. We do not in any way whatsoever warrant or guarantee the success of any action you take based on statements or information available in this book. Past performance is not necessarily indicative of future results. All investments carry significant risk, and all investment decisions remain the specific responsibility of the individual. There is no guarantee that systems, indicators, or signals will result in profits or that they will not result in full or partial losses. All investors are advised to fully understand all risks associated with any kind of investing they choose to do.

2

Welcome!

Who is this book for?

This book is for anyone who is looking to get started in the world of investing and wants to learn about straightforward approaches that almost anyone can understand. I believe the world of investing doesn't have to be complicated and doesn't have to be dangerous. Yes, of course, there is risk in any investment, but we can mitigate these risks by understanding our investments and keeping the process simple. The earlier you start with safe investing, the more you will reap the rewards of time.

"The best time to plant a tree was 20 years ago. The second best time is today"

- Chinese Proverb

What are Shares of a Company?

A share of a company is a unit of ownership in that company. When a company goes public and begins to trade on the stock market, they are initially split up into a certain amount of shares. This amount varies for every company and can be a vast difference. In this book, I will attempt to show you real-life examples of stocks to make this easier for you. Here is an example of a company being split into shares.

Example:

The Coca-Cola Company currently has around 4,310,000,000 shares that are being traded on the open market. That means that the company is broken up into 4.3 Billion units that we call 'Shares'. These shares are almost continuously being bought and sold on the stock market anytime the markets are open. **Bulls** (Buyers who think the stock is going to rise in price) and **Bears** (Sellers who think the stock is going to fall in price) are always trading popular company stocks and this is what fluctuates the price of a stock. This is why it is said that the stock market is simply an auction house that sells small pieces of companies.

Again the amount of shares traded varies for every company, but don't get caught up on that right now. The chance of one person buying all of a company, especially a significantly large company is not a common thing.

Regular Market Hours:
  New York Stock Exchange (NYSE) and NASDAQ
  9:30 AM to 4:00 PM Eastern Time (ET), Monday through Friday.
  Markets are closed on weekends and certain holidays.

(I Do however believe that soon we will have a 24/7 Stock Market. This is just a personal Guess, not yet a fact.)

WELCOME!

What are dividends?

In simple terms, a dividend is a payment made by a corporation to its shareholders, usually in cash, as a portion of the company's profits. Usually, these payments are made quarterly (every 3 months) and will be deposited directly into your brokerage account. Don't worry if you don't have a brokerage account yet, or don't know what that is. I'll explain brokerage accounts later in this book.

Why should I invest in dividend-paying companies?

In many cases, but not always, the paying of dividends by a company indicates better health for that company. The reason for this is that dividends are paid out of profits that are made by the good choices of the CEO and Heads of the company. Some things that the consistent and ever-increasing payment of dividends suggests are that:

- **That the company is generating enough profit to distribute some of that to its shareholders**

- **It can indicate that the company has stable cash flow and that they are sound when it comes to company finances.**

- **It can show that the management has confidence in the company and its future earnings**

- **Many times a company that pays dividends is more mature, unlike a new company that may be re-investing its profits into the growth of the company**

I'm sure you've heard stories of someone making a million dollars on a one thousand-dollar crypto investment, but I assure you many have lost all of their investments in the newest and latest crypto or penny stock. That's not to say that no one should invest in crypto or penny stocks, but just to iterate the fact that I believe you should understand what you are investing in. You don't have to be a professional in the industry, but at least have a general understanding of what the company does and what it creates. When it comes to dividend stocks, you can find them in all shapes, sizes, and industries, but that doesn't mean that they are all worth investing in. We want to be smart about our investing and put our money where it brings in a meaningful return on investment (ROI), while also being reasonably safe. To achieve this we will have to do some research to find companies that pay dividends, and that fit into our criteria as a good investment. In upcoming chapters, we will go over things like Criteria, ROI, Research, Charts, Brokerage accounts, qualified vs. non-qualified dividends, Ticker symbols, and some more resources that will make managing your portfolio easier. As I said before, we should keep this process as simple as possible without harming the quality of our portfolio.

In the next chapter, we'll talk about how dividends work, and head into opening a brokerage account, free research tools, and more.

3

How do Dividends Work

Most dividend stocks pay out quarterly, which as you probably well know is every three months. In the world of dividend stocks, there is a certain day that is called the "**Ex-Dividend date**". This date is exactly 1 day before the "**Date of Record**" and usually 2-4 weeks before the actual **dividend payment**. Let's take a deeper look at this with a real-life example.

Example:

One company that is very popular among dividend investors and the great Warren Buffet is "**Coca-Cola**" at the time of this writing Coca-Cola has an upcoming dividend payment of 0.485 cents per share and here is how the dates work:

Ex-Dividend Date, June 14th:

Anyone who owns shares of Coca-Cola when the market opens on

June 14th will receive the upcoming dividend for any shares that they own. Anyone buying on or after this date will not receive the upcoming dividend, but if they hold onto the stock until the next Ex-dividend date (3 months), they would then receive that dividend payment. The Ex-dividend date falls 1 day before the DATE OF RECORD.

Date of Record, June 15th:

This is the cutoff date established by a company to determine which shareholders are eligible to receive a dividend payment on the upcoming dividend payment date. To be on the record books on this day, you will have needed to purchase the stock before the Ex-Dividend Date mentioned above.

Pay Date, July 1st:

As I mentioned before, the pay date is approximately two to four weeks after the Ex-Dividend Date. The pay date is usually when you will see the dividend payment appear in your brokerage account.

Amount paid:

The amount that you receive depends on how many shares of the company you own. We talked about shares earlier.

For Example:

Dave owns 1 share of Coca-Cola and the current dividend is $0.485 per share. That means that Dave will receive:

$$\$0.485 \times 1 \text{ share} = \$0.485$$

Of course, that was extremely easy math, but as you accumulate more shares through continuous investing it will become more like this:

Example

Dave owns 128 shares of Coca-Cola and the current dividend is $0.485

Cents per share. That means Dave will receive:

$$\$0.485 \times 128 = \$62.08$$

Simply put, the more you own, the more passive income you will receive from your investment. In other words, you are buying passive income with active income. We'll go into this later in the book in the chapter dedicated to passive income.

Now that you know a little about how Dividends work and are calculated we are going to move on and talk about Brokerage accounts. Opening a brokerage account is one of the first steps of investing in dividend stocks if you plan on doing it yourself instead of hiring an investment advisor.

4

What is a Brokerage account?

The words "brokerage account" may sound fancy, but in reality, all a brokerage account does is allow you to buy stocks from someone who wants to sell them, or sell stocks to someone who wants to buy them. You have to understand that for every share of stock that one person sells, someone else is buying that same share that was sold. Like I said, the stock market is an auction house.

In essence, a brokerage account bridges the gap between buyers and sellers without you ever having to talk to the other person. This wasn't always the case though. Before the technological advancements that we see today, there was a completely different method of buying stocks of companies.

In those days, you would have to either call or visit your stock broker in person, give them the information about the stock that you are interested in buying, and then give them the criteria that the stock must meet before you are willing to buy it. Criteria can be things such as stock prices, news events, and chart patterns. Without the technological advancements that we have nowadays, there wouldn't be any self-directed investors. Thankfully we have the means to buy and sell stocks directly from our computer or even our cell phone.

We will talk more about stock criteria and self-directed investing later in the book.

In summary, a brokerage account simply allows you to buy and sell stocks without ever having to talk to another person, all from the comfort of your home, office, car, or pretty much anywhere that you have a connection to the internet.

How do I find a brokerage to use?

Finding a brokerage to use doesn't have to be complicated, but there are a few things that you should look for in a brokerage:

- Dependability
- Well-known and established company
- Trustworthy
- A large variety of stocks available
- User-friendly function
- Low or no fees

Finding a brokerage that meets these guidelines should give you a good foundation for building your portfolio. Keep in mind that you can usually transfer your stock holdings to another brokerage if you decide that you don't like the one you start with. This sometimes costs money and can be a little complicated, but many times it is an option. I will list a few of my favorite brokerage accounts below, but you should always do your own research before making any decisions.

Before I make the list I want to point out that in times past, a person would have to pay a transaction/commission fee every time they bought or sold stocks. Usually, this fee was around $6.95. This all changed around 2015 when a company called **Robinhood** was created and began offering commission-free trading to all of its users. When they began this, it put pressure on the other major players in the industry. If you fast forward to today, you will find that almost every brokerage you see will be offering commission-free trades. This changes if you start trading stocks that are called **"OTC" (Over the counter),** which means that they are not listed on any major stock exchange. Many times these are smaller/newer companies or penny stocks and you may still have to pay a fee to trade those stocks. Now on to my list, and I will start with none other than Robinhood itself.

- **Robinhood**

I dare to say Robinhood has possibly become one of the most popular brokerage accounts in America among new investors. They offer a huge variety of stocks and boast a very user-friendly platform. Though they lack somewhat in research availability, I would rate Robinhood as one of the top on my list for ease of use when it comes to new investors.

WHAT IS A BROKERAGE ACCOUNT?

- **Schwab (Formerly known as TD Ameritrade)**

I personally liked them better when they were TD Ameritrade, but they are still a good brokerage. They are a big name in the investment industry and I have also personally used them. They are not as user-friendly as Robinhood, but they offer a lot more in the way of research availability, and stock news. Overall I still think they're a good option myself.

- **Webull**

Webull came along a few years after Robinhood and it too was intended to be a brokerage for the new investor. My experience with Webull is limited, but in the time that I have spent using it, I found it to be much less user-friendly than Robinhood. I'm sure with practice I might like it better, but first impressions didn't sit well with me as far as design goes. That being said it is a very popular brokerage and you have probably seen ads for it in the past.

- **Fidelity**

Fidelity is a big player in the industry right beside Schwab as I mentioned earlier. I don't have personal experience with fidelity, but it might be something you want to research.

- **E*TRADE**

The same as Fidelity, I don't have any experience with this brokerage, but they are very well known and something you should at least look at during your research.

Now that you have 5 of the most popular brokerages that I know of, you should do your own research and see if one of them is right for your needs. Who knows, you may run across another brokerage that you like better than any of these.

How do I open a brokerage account?

Every brokerage is going to be a little different when it comes to opening an account. For example, I am going to walk you through the steps to open a Robinhood account and a Schwab account the best that I can. To open an account and buy stocks, you are going to need a bank account. I'm sure that you already know this, but I'm trying to be thorough with my instructions.

Opening a Robinhood Account:

There will be a lot of questions asked by Robinhood, but keep in mind that they are legally required to ask these questions, as stock trading is a highly regulated industry by the SEC.

If you don't feel comfortable, with the question you can always talk to a financial advisor about the process.

WHAT IS A BROKERAGE ACCOUNT?

- Go to the Robinhood website, or use the Robinhood app.

- Click on the SIGN-UP button

- Create your login: First name, last name, email address, and create a password. Now Click Continue. Make sure that you put your name just as it appears on your government-issued identification. Robinhood will use this to verify your identity.

- Verify your identity: Phone number and address. Then they will send you a confirmation code by call or text, depending on what you choose. Enter the code that you receive and hit submit.

- They will now ask for your Social Security number, date of birth, and citizenship.

- Now it is going to ask you a few questions about investing:

- How much investing experience do you have?

- Would you like to enable commission-free "**Options**" trading? **(If you don't know what options are, you can click learn more, but they are much more complicated than regular stocks and we won't go into them in this book).**

- Now it will ask questions about employment.

- Now it will ask if you or a family member are a senior executive, or 10% shareholder at a publicly traded company. For most people, this is a No.

- Now it will ask if you or any of your family members work for a stock exchange or brokerage. For most people, this is also No.

- Now you will have to review the tax certification and sign some agreements. Make sure to read everything so that you know if you are okay with the agreements and that you have all of your information correct.

- Now it will take you to the page to link your bank account. You will have to do this to fund your account and buy stocks.

WHAT IS A BROKERAGE ACCOUNT?

- After linking your account it will take you to the page to make your first deposit. You can start with as little as $1. The amount is completely up to you, and your budgeting.

That's it! As long as everything was confirmed correctly, you should have a Robinhood account. In the case that they needed to verify some of the information, it could take a couple of days. If you run into any problems, you can contact Robinhood customer support, and they should be able to help you get through the issue.

We will move on to opening a Schwab account now. The process will be very similar, but there could be a couple of different steps. Keep in mind that you don't have to open both accounts. You can always try one of them and if you don't like it, come back to the book and open the other.

Opening a Schwab Account

- Navigate to Schwab.com

- click on "OPEN ACCOUNT"

- select 'Individual Brokerage'

- Click 'Get Started'

- Now you will need to fill out your personal information: First name, Last name, and address, Date of birth, Social security number, Email, and Phone number. Then select Continue.

- Now it will let you add a trusted contact. You can fill this out or skip it.

- Now it will ask you general questions about why you are opening the account. You can enter this information and then select Continue.

- It should now ask for your employment status. You can enter this and then hit continue.

- Just as Robinhood did, it will now ask you questions about you or your family working for a brokerage, or being a senior executive. After answering these questions, hit continue. The next few questions should be about paperless documents, Schwab agreements, and then some trading options. It will ask you about options trading, and Margin trading.

As I stated before, I won't be going into options trading in this book due to its complexity. **I highly suggest staying away from margin trading!**

At this point, you should now have a Schwab account opened. After opening you will have the option to link bank accounts and fund your account. As I have said before, Schwab is more difficult to use than Robinhood but offers more research and stock information. With some practice, I'm sure you will get the hang of it. In the next chapter, we will talk more about types of passive income streams, Return on investment, and Qualified vs. Non-qualified stock dividend payments. If you have already opened your account, feel free to play around with it. Don't feel rushed to put money inside and buy stocks. Become comfortable with the platform and learn how to navigate it well.

5

What is passive income?

You can think of passive income as an income earned without your active involvement, or at least with minimal effort. I like to say that I buy passive income with my active income, but in truth, I buy passive income with my active income and more passive income with the passive income that I already make from the previous investment. Now I know that probably sounded a little confusing, but I'll explain it much better a little later.

Types of Passive Income:

1. **Stocks**
2. **Real estate**
3. **Loan investing**
4. **CD's**
5. **High-interest savings account**
6. **Non-personally managed business**

Stocks:

As you probably know by now, this book is specifically written for stock investing; more specifically, dividend stocks. Companies pay dividends out of the profits from the company, but not all companies pay dividends. Many times for smaller or newer companies it is more beneficial to reinvest the money into the growth of the company, and that can also be a good thing for the shareholders. As a company grows profitably and in size, many times the stock price grows with it.

Real Estate:

Real estate is a whole different industry and though many people call their income from rents passive, I would dare to say no. I have a substantial amount of experience in real estate and though there is a lot of money to be made, there is a lot of work to be put out. One of the only ways that I consider real estate to be passive is if you own a building such as an apartment complex and pay a management company to manage it. Even in this case, you would have to ensure that the property brings in enough profit to be able to afford the management company and any required maintenance.

All of this being said I have invested in real estate, I am currently investing in real estate, and I will continue to invest in real estate in the future. From my experience, however, I do not consider it to be a form of true passive income.

Loan investing:

There are too many ways of investing in loans, or 'Debt investing' to list them all here, so I will list the top 3 that I know of:

Peer-2-Peer Lending:

You can do a web search of Peer-2-Peer lending and you will see many companies appear. These companies simply connect borrowers (People who need money) to lenders (People who have money). You, as a lender would loan money to a borrower, and you would receive your money back in payments along with any interest that you may have earned on the loan.

Real estate Crowdfunding:

For this option, you put your money in with other investors to finance a real estate deal for a borrower. I don't have much experience in this area, so I'm not going to go very deep into the topic. Feel free to give it a Google search and see what you can find out for yourself.

Private Lending:

Private lending is just what it sounds like. You, loaning your money to a sole individual for them to usually make some type of large purchase or investment of their own. **This can be very risky!** I personally do not do this type of lending specifically because of the risk. Maybe if I looked into it more I wouldn't be so weary of it, but until then I think I'll keep avoiding it.

This should give you an idea of the options for passive income, but as I said before, there are many ways to make this type of income and I have just scratched the surface.

We are going to get back on track and jump right back into dividend investing by talking a little about ROI (Return on Investment).

What is ROI and how to calculate it for stocks?

Here is a simple example of Return on Investment (ROI):

Example

Dave is a dividend investor and decides to buy 1 share of Coca-Cola. Coca-Cola pays a dividend of 0.485 cents per share, every quarter of the year. That comes to a yearly total of $1.94 per share. At the current stock price of $62.84 per share.

This means that for every $62.84 that you invest in Coca-Cola, you will make $1.94 per year. This comes out to a return on investment (ROI) of 3.08%

This is not the highest-paying stock available, but I am using it as an example because it is such a popular company and a popular dividend stock.

In summary:

ROI is the amount of money you make, from the amount of money you invested. There's no use in overcomplicating things, especially in the beginning as a new investor.

Qualified VS. Non-Qualified Dividends

In the upcoming chapters, we will begin talking about stock research, charts, and free resources that you can use to decide which companies you would like to invest in. Before that, I would like to end this chapter with a short discussion about qualified and non-qualified dividend stocks.

Qualified Dividends and what they are:

Qualified dividends that meet certain requirements are taxed at a lower capital gain tax. Whereas ordinary dividends are taxed as normal income which is usually significantly higher. The lower capital gains tax bracket is currently at 0%, 15%, and 20% depending on which tax bracket your total income falls into. There are normally three requirements for a dividend to be considered qualified:

The dividend must be paid by a U.S. corporation or some type of qualifying foreign entity:

This could be companies incorporated in U.S. possession or corporations that are included in foreign tax treaties with the U.S.

It has to be considered a regular dividend in the eyes of the IRS:

This means that it has to be an ordinary dividend, not something that is actually an interest payment from a bank or credit union, or a premium paid back by an insurance company

You have to have owned the stock for "Long Enough" the time frame called the holding period:

You must hold the stock shares for at least 60 days during the 121-day period, and this period begins 60 days before the ex-dividend date. So if an ex-dividend date is on June 1st, the 121-day period would have started on April 2nd (60 days before ex-dividend) and ended on August 1st. You would have needed to own the stock for 60 days within that time frame, and of course, owned it before the ex-dividend date.

A couple of easy ways that you can figure out if a company qualifies for these types of dividends are:

- Contact the investor relations department of a company and they should definitely be able to give you this information.

- Visit the company's investor relations web page. Much of this information is readily available online.

- Consult a Tax Attorney and they will be able to guide you in the right path.

6

How to find stocks that pay dividends:

There are many simple ways to find dividend-paying stocks, a few of which I will put in this list below:

- **A Google search** of the company name or ticker symbol should give you a quick way of finding information about a stock. (A ticker symbol is what stock exchanges use to identify a certain stock. For example: Coca-Cola has a ticker symbol of 'KO' and carnival cruise lines have a ticker symbol of 'CCL').

- **Yahoo Finance** is a good source of information about stocks and investments. It's so useful to me that I'm going to give you an example of how to search for dividend stocks using it.

HOW TO FIND STOCKS THAT PAY DIVIDENDS:

Example

- Navigate to https://finance.yahoo.com

- On the menu bar, Click "SCREENERS"

- In the box, click on "Create New Screener"

- In the pop-up window click "Equity"

- In the 'build stock screener window, click on "Add another filter"

- In the pop-up window search bar, type in dividend.

- Now check the box beside "Consecutive years of dividend growth"

- Click the "Close" button

- Now, in the box beside the words "Consecutive Years of Dividend Growth greater than" type in 1.

- Click "Find Stocks"

You should now see a massive list of stocks that pay dividends, and be able to see information about the stocks. If you click on the ticker symbol on the left of any of the line items it will take you to a page that is all about that certain stock. This can be a very useful tool when looking for stocks that have paid a consistent and ever-increasing dividend for a large number of years. You can adjust the number of years in the filter to be however many you want it to be, I played with it and the longest amount of years I found was Johnston and Johnston. According to Yahoo Finance, they have been paying an ever-increasing dividend for 60 years.

- **Dividend.com** is a resource that I use to see the history of a dividend stock. It shows me how many years a stock has been paying dividends, how much it pays, and any increase or decrease in dividend payments. you can just search the stock in the website's search bar.

HOW TO FIND STOCKS THAT PAY DIVIDENDS:

- **Nasdaq.com** is a good source of information on stocks and dividend stocks. You can just search for the company name or ticker symbol in the web page search bar.

After reading this book, I would suggest going to some of the resources that I list and learning your way around the sites and apps. The better you are at navigating your tools, the easier it will be when you get ready to do research and invest. Next, we will talk about 'Stock Criteria'.

Stock Criteria:

Stock criteria are simply the requirements that a stock must meet for us to be interested in owning it. Everyone has different criteria depending on what their investment goals are. Some people are looking for growth stocks, others are looking for income stocks (dividends), and some are looking for a mixture of both in their portfolios. I'm not going to tell you what your criteria should be, but instead, share with you my criteria for educational purposes.

My criteria consists of only a few items:

- **I want the company to have paid consecutive dividends for at least the past 20 years. This is the year 2024, which would mean that the company was strong enough to pay dividends through the 2008 recession and the COVID-19 pandemic.**

- I want the company's dividend yield to be at least 4%. This means that I would be making at least a 4% return on my investment. I prefer for it to be closer to 6%, but unless I really like the company, 4% is my minimum.

- I want the average daily trading volume to be high enough that I will never have a problem selling the stock if I decide to. The daily trading volume is simply how many shares were bought or sold in a single day, for example, Coca-Cola has an average daily trading volume of nearly 13 million shares. That's plenty of volume that I feel comfortable being able to sell if I ever wanted to.

- The dividend has to be a Qualified Dividend, We talked about this earlier. The reason I want this is to lower my tax liability.

- Last but not least, I want to do a Google search of the company and make sure that there are no devastating news articles recently posted. These could be anything like lawsuits, bankruptcy, Mass recalls, or anything else that could damage a company beyond repair.

There are also 2 lists that I look through every time I start to look for an investment, that is the **Dividend Kings list** and the **Dividend**

HOW TO FIND STOCKS THAT PAY DIVIDENDS:

Aristocrats list. I am going to give more information and the full list in the next chapter. Now you should do some research and try to come up with your own criteria for stock investing depending on what goals you want to reach. Next, we will talk about charts.

Charts, what they are, and how to use them:

Charts give you a visual, and graphical representation of a stock's price over the course of a specified timeline. It can be represented with a simple line graph, candlestick chart (My favorite), or bar chart. The easiest to understand as a beginner is probably the line graph and to be honest, as a long-term dividend investor, I don't use a chart as much as if I were buying and selling every week like swing traders.

For my charts, I use a free website called "Trading View". They offer a great free charting service, stock news, stock ideas, and a whole lot more. Here is an example of how to use them.

Example

- **Navigate to https://www.tradingview.com/**

(I would suggest signing up for a free account to save watch lists and things like that, but that is totally up to you.)

- **In the search bar type in a company or ticker symbol, for this example I am typing in (KO), the ticker symbol for Coca-Cola.**

- The company name popped up in a drop-down window along with a lot of other names. If you are in America and looking for American stock for this company, it will usually be the one with the American flag beside it.

- Click on it and it will take you to the page for the company on Tradingview, and you should see a lot of information on the company. Look around and see what you can find.

- Now, in order to open up the charts for this company I am going to click on the button that says "see on Super Charts in the top right"

- A new browser tab should open and you will see a chart for the stock that you selected.

- On the top of the chart there are multiple things you can select, time frame, graph type, indicators, and on the left side of the screen there drawing tools.

I would suggest going on to YouTube and watching some videos on stock chart reading. Though I am pretty good at reading and explaining charts, it would be a whole other book in itself due to the massive amount of indicators, chart patterns, and options available to you.

I simply wanted to give you an overview and not overwhelm you with information that you should gain over time, not in the course of one book.

Of course, this is not the only place to get stock charts, but for what I need it is more than enough. Feel free to look around and see what you can find in the world of charts. I will provide a resource list at the end of the book that you can reference.

7

Dividend Kings and Aristocrats

These are prestigious classes of stocks known for their consistent and ever-increasing dividends. They are split into two classes and here is an explanation of the two:

Dividend Kings:

- Dividend Kings are companies that have increased their dividends every year for at least 50 consecutive years.

- Achieving this milestone indicates financial strength and a strong commitment to returning profits to your shareholders.

- It shows the potential for long-term, reliable dividend payments.

- Usually points to a strong company.

- Usually seen as a safer investment during turbulent times.

Dividend Aristocrats:

- Dividend Aristocrats are companies that have increased their dividends every year for at least 25 consecutive years.

- This status demonstrates a solid history of dividend growth and indicates a company's strength and stability.

- Consistent Dividend Growth.

- Well Established Company.

There are usually fewer dividend kings due to the length of time requirements. Both are still a very prestigious group of companies that usually offer income stability, good financial health, and investments that tend to perform better in uncertain economic times. I am going to provide a list of the current Kings and Aristocrats below, but be aware that **this list changes from year to year** depending on company decisions. The list will have the company name, the ticker symbol in parenthesis, and the number of years that they have been paying increasing dividends in this order.

** These lists are for educational purposes only and have been compiled with the most accurate information that I could find at the time. These Lists change regularly. I believe them to be correct, but you should verify this information for yourself. Never make financial decisions without consulting a professional. **

Current Dividend Kings 2024

1. **American States Water (AWR) 69 Years**
2. **Dover Corporation (DOV) 68 Years**
3. **Northwest Natural Holdings (NWN) 68 Years**
4. **Genuine Parts (GPC) 68 Years**
5. **Parker Hannifin (PH) 68 Years**
6. **Proctor and Gamble (PG) 68 Years**
7. **Emerson Electric (EMR) 67 Years**
8. **Cincinnati Financial (CINF) 63 Years**

DIVIDEND KINGS AND ARISTOCRATS

9. Coca-Cola (KO) 62 Years
10. Johnson and Johnson (JNJ) 62 Years
11. Kenvue (KVUE) 61
12. Lancaster Colony (LANC) 61 years
13. Colgate Palmolive (CL) 61 Years
14. Nordson (NDSN) 60 Years
15. Farmers and Merchants Bancorp (FMCB) 59 Years
16. Hormel Foods (HRL) 58 Years
17. ABM Industries (ABM) 57 Years
18. California Water Service Group (CWT) 57 Years
19. Federal Realty Investment Trust (FRT) 56 Years
20. Stanley Black and Decker (SWK) 56 Years
21. Commerce Bancshares (CBSH) 56 Years
22. SJW Group (SJW) 56 Years
23. Stepan (SCL) 56 Years
24. H.B. Fuller (FUL) 55 Years
25. Sysco (SYY) 55 Years
26. Altria Group (MO) 54 Years
27. MSA Safety (MSA) 54 Years
28. Black Hills Corporation (BKH) 54 Years
29. Illinois Tool Works (ITW)
30. National Fuel Gas (NFG) 53 Years
31. Universal Corporation (UVV) 53 Years
32. W.W. Grainger (GWW) 53 Years
33. AbbVie (ABBV) 52 Years
34. Becton, Dickinson & co. (BDX) 52 Years
35. PPG Industries (PPG) 52 Years
36. Target (TGT) 52 Years
37. Tennant (TNC) 52 Years
38. Canadian Utilities (CDUAF) 52 Years
39. Abbott Labs (ABT) 52 Years

40. **Kimberly Clark (KMB) 52 Years**
41. **PepsiCo (PEP) 52 Years**
42. **Lowe's (LOW) 51 Years**
43. **Nucor (NUE) 51 Years**
44. **The Gorman Rupp Company (GRC) 51 Years**
45. **Tootsie Roll Industries (TR) 51 Years**
46. **ADM (ADM) 51 Years**
47. **S&P Global (SPGI) 51 Years**
48. **Wal-Mart (WMT) 51 Years**
49. **Fortis Inc. (FTS) 50 Years**
50. **Middlesex Water (MSEX) 50 Years**
51. **RPM International (RPM) 50 Years**
52. **United Bankshares (UBSI) 50 Years**

Keep in mind that these lists change as time goes on, either from a company stopping their dividend increases or another company being added because of making the requirements. Though it is very rare for a company of this strength to stop increasing, it could happen. After reaching this status, most companies would not want to have to start over from the beginning because being in this prestigious class attracts many investors who are looking for income and safety.

Current Dividend Aristocrats 2024

1. **Archer-Daniels-Midland Co. (ADM) 48 Years**
2. **Automatic Data Processing (ADP) 48 Years**

DIVIDEND KINGS AND ARISTOCRATS

3. Aflac Inc. (AFL) 42 Years
4. Albemarle (ALB) 29 Years
5. Amcor (AMCR) 28 Years
6. Smith A.O. Corp. (AOS) 30 Years
7. Air Products and chemicals (APD) 41 Years
8. Atmos Energy (ATO) 40 Years
9. Franklin Resources Inc. (BEN) 44 Years
10. Brown-Foreman Corp B (BF.B) 39 Years
11. Brown & Brown (BRO) 30 Years
12. Cardinal Health Inc. (CAH) 27 Years
13. Caterpillar Inc. (CAT) 30 Years
14. Chubb LTD (CB) 30 Years
15. Church and Dwight (CHD) 27 Years
16. C.H. Robinson Worldwide (CHRW) 26 Years
17. Clorox Co (CLX) 46 Years
18. Cintas Corp. (CTAS) 41 Years
19. Chevron Corp. (CVX) 36 Years
20. Ecolab Inc. (ECL) 32 Years
21. Consolidated Edison (ED) 46 Years
22. Essex Property Trust (ESS) 29 Years
23. Expeditors International (EXPD) 29 Years
24. Fastenal (FAST) 25 Years
25. General Dynamics (GD) 32 Years
26. International business machines (IBM) 28 Years
27. Linde PLC (LIN) 30 Years
28. McDonald's Corp. (MCD) 48 Years
29. Medtronic PLC (MDT) 46 Years
30. McCormick & Co. (MKC) 37 Years
31. NextEra Energy (NEE) 29 Years
32. Realty Income Corp. (O) 31 Years
33. Pentair PLC (PNR 48 Years

34. Roper Technologies (ROP) 31 Years
35. Sherwin Williams (SHW) 45 Years
36. J.M. Smucker (SJM) 26 Years
37. T. Rowe Price Group Inc. (TROW) 37 Years
38. West Pharmaceuticals Services (WST) 31 Years
39. Exxon Mobile Corp. (XOM) 41 Years

**These lists are for educational purposes only and have been compiled with the most accurate information that I could find at the time. These Lists change regularly. I believe them to be correct, but you should verify this information for yourself. **

8

The Power of Compound Interest

"*Compound interest is the eighth wonder of the world. He who understands it, earns it; he who doesn't, pays it.*"

• *Attributed to* **Albert Einstein**

What is Compound Interest?

Compound interest is best described as a snowball effect. For example, you have your initial principal, the interest rate that you earn on your money, and the timeframe for which your investment compounds (For us, most stocks compound quarterly). Every time that you earn interest on the original investment and add it to the principle, the initial investment gets larger, therefore earning more interest on the next quarter payment. Let me try and give you an example.

Example

Dave buys $1,000 of the stock AT&T which has a dividend yield of around 6% and pays dividends quarterly. Below you will see the compound interest at work in every quarter. This will be calculated at the 6% dividend yield. With good research, 6% is an achievable ROI.

Quarter	Total investment	Dividend this quarter	New total investment
1	$1,000	$15	$1,015
2	$1,015	$15.22	$1,030.22
3	$1,030.22	$15.45	$1,045.67
4	1,045.67	$15.68	$1,061.35
5	$1,061.35	$15.92	$1,077.27
6	$1,077.27	$16.15	$1,093.42
7	$1,093.42	$16.40	$1,109.82
8	$1,109.82	$16.64	$1,126.46
9	$1,126.46	$16.89	$1,143.35
10	$1,143.35	$17.15	$1,160.50
11	$1,160.50	$17.40	$1,177.90
12	$1,177.90	$17.66	$1,195.56
13	$1,195.56	$17.93	$1,213.49
14	$1,213.49	$18.20	1,231.69
15	$1,231.69	$18.47	$1,250.16

You can see the effect of compound interest in this chart. This chart is very simple, as you can have many more variables in the stock market. If you continuously invest more into your positions on a weekly or monthly basis it can significantly increase the snowball effect. You also have to take into account the rise or fall in the price of the underlying stock. If you want to play around with compound interest, you can find a lot of compound interest calculators online that are free to use.

DRIP: Dividend Re-investment Plan

What is drip?

Drip, or (Dividend Re-investment plan) is an option with both of the brokerage accounts that I walked you through the setup on (Robinhood and Schwab). This allows you to automatically re-invest your dividend income into the stocks you received it from without having to do it yourself. When you receive your dividend payment into your brokerage account, it will automatically buy more shares of the stock, either in whole shares or fractional shares. Yes, it can buy fractions of a share if there is not enough money to buy a whole share. When it comes to fractional shares, you will still receive a fraction of the dividend in relation to the amount of the fractional share. Here's an example:

Example of fractional shares and their dividend income

Dave owns 10 shares of Coca-Cola and should be receiving his dividend today. Dave has also selected the drip feature on his brokerage account, so the dividend he receives will automatically be reinvested back into Coca-Cola. Here is what that process looks like:

Coca-Cola pays Dave $0.49 per share this quarter of the year for a total of $4.90. Considering the stock currently costs $63.59 per share, the

DRIP won't be able to buy a whole share of the stock. Instead, DRIP buys as much of one share as it can with the dividend, resulting in Dave having a partial share in his account. After DRIP has done its job Dave now owns 10.07 shares of Coca-Cola. This is how DRIP works in your brokerage account.

How Do I Track My Investments?

I try to keep the tracking of my investments very simple and to the point. I don't want to complicate the process any more than is necessary, as the stock market and investing are already confusing enough as it is. So here are a few ways I track my investments:

- Having a hard copy of my investments by logging everything in a trading journal.

- Having a digital copy of my investments. This can be my brokerage account holdings, or you can make some type of Word document for this.

- I keep an Excel spreadsheet with my investments listed inside and create columns that calculate my yearly, monthly, and daily dividend income. This part may sound complicated, but with a little basic math and knowledge of Excel, it is pretty simple.

- **Another option is dividend tracking apps that sync with your brokerage account and track all of your dividends. I do not use these, as they are usually pricey.** I will say that if you decide to use one, make sure that it is a reliable company. After all, you will be syncing your brokerage account to it and that has sensitive information.

Don't overcomplicate it. Find the way that best suits you, and as you start there is really no need for expensive tracking software. In most people's cases, you are not starting with hundreds of thousands of dollars and that's okay. When I started, I was putting 5 dollars a day into my investment account. Whatever you start with, you should just be proud that you started, and are striving for a better future.

K.I.S.S Method (Keep it Stupid Simple)

I've heard this saying since I was a kid and I never forgot it. It's simply reiterating that if you keep the process simple, in most cases it will be more efficient and run much smoother than if it's designed by a rocket scientist. So as you are building your own strategies and portfolios, don't make it harder than it has to be. Conduct good research, talk to good professionals, make good decisions, and don't invest money you can't afford to lose. For some people, it might not be the right time to start buying stocks. For example, if it's going to cause you to miss paying your bills you would be better off waiting until you are in a more favorable financial situation to start investing. I know that waiting is not ideal, because when it comes to dividends and the snowball effect they have, time literally is money. On the other hand, you don't want to live your life in stress and fear of not being able to pay your bills because of buying stocks.

9

Self-Directed Investors

A simple explanation of Self-directed investors is that they make their own investment decisions and manage their own portfolios without relying on the help of financial advisors or brokers. They will conduct their own research and stock analysis while choosing where they want to invest their money. I personally am a self-directed investor, but I always suggest that you talk to a financial advisor before starting on your investment journey. In the beginning, there are so many options, questions, and investment opportunities that it can get confusing.

Pros of Self-directed Investing:

- In control: You have complete control of your investment portfolio and decisions. **(Depending on knowledge and discipline, this can also be a con.)**

- Saves Money: By being self-directed, you eliminate the fees that would come with an advisor or broker.

- You can adjust your strategy to meet your specific needs and risk tolerance.

- Done correctly, it can be a great educational opportunity and give you a much deeper understanding of what you are investing your hard-earned money into.

- You can make decisions on your own time, faster or slower without waiting for approval from anyone.

Cons of Self-Directed Investing:

- Time: Managing and researching a portfolio can consume a lot of your time, especially in the beginning.

- Lack of experience: Without experience, it can be difficult to understand what's going on with the markets, and sometimes you may end up in a state of analysis paralysis.

- Responsibility: As I said in the pros section, **you have complete control of your investment portfolio and decisions.** Depending on a lot of things like experience, discipline, time availability, and many other things, this too could cause a problem.

Portfolio managers/Investment advisors

These are the people who assist investors in the buying selling research and pretty much every aspect of investing. Some of the things that they do for you are:

- They develop and help you implement an investment strategy that fits your goals, such as growth stocks, income stocks, and the risk management of your portfolio.

- They regularly monitor the performance of your investment portfolio and communicate back and forth with you, the customer.

- They offer investment advice, education, and market research.

Advisors and portfolio managers can play a critical role in helping clients achieve their investment goals. Advisors offer a broader spectrum of financial advice, whereas portfolio managers typically focus more on the day-to-day operation of the investments.

All of this being said, I once again suggest that you talk to professionals before making a decision. Though it might seem tempting to go it alone to save fees and have control, if done incorrectly, it can end up costing you more money than the fees would have.

10

Resources that may help you in your investment journey.

Brokerages:

- **Robinhood**
- **E*trade**
- **Schwab**
- **Fidelity**
- **Merrill Edge**

Chart options, Free:

- TradingView
- Yahoo Finance
- Google Finance
- Market Watch
- Investing.com
- StockCharts

Chart options, Paid:

- Bloomberg Terminal
- MetaStock
- eSignal
- TradeStation
- Think or Swim
- NinjaTrader

Research:

- TradingView
- Yahoo Finance
- Google Finance
- Bloomberg
- Dividend.com
- MarketWatch
- SeekingAlpha
- MorningStar
- Zacks investment research
- Most brokerage accounts have some research capabilities.

11

Conclusion:

In conclusion, investing doesn't have to be overly complicated and scary. With the right knowledge and professional help, anyone can start planning for a better future and a stronger retirement. I hope you take the time to find, and talk to an investment advisor about your own retirement outlook and see where exactly you stand.

"The best time to plant a tree was 20 years ago. The second best time is today"

- Chinese proverb

I hope that through the course of this book, you found something that was useful and informative. It has been my pleasure sharing my investment knowledge with you and I wish you the best on this journey. If you found any useful information in this book, Please leave us a favorable review. It helps out more than you could ever know.

Until next time, Invest safely and wisely.

Thanks!!

www.ingramcontent.com/pod-product-compliance
Lightning Source LLC
Chambersburg PA
CBHW071959210526
45479CB00003B/996